Cover Photo: Angolan Peach-faced Lovebird
Endpapers: *Left*-Black-cheeked Lovebird
             Right-Abyssinian Lovebird hen

HOWELL
Beginner's guide to
Lovebirds

David Alderton M.A.

Editor
Dennis Kelsey-Wood

HOWELL BOOK HOUSE Inc.
230 Park Avenue
New York, N.Y. 10169

Library of Congress Cataloging-in-Publication Data

ALderton, David 1956-
Howell beginner's guide to lovebirds.

Summary: A basic guide to the care of lovebirds, covering such aspects as feeding, breeding, exhibition, and health problems.
1. Lovebirds—Juvenile literature. [1. Lovebirds.
2. Birds] I. Title. II. Title: Lovebirds.
SF473.L6A43   1985   636.6'865   85-18130
ISBN 0-87605-936-1

Book design by Routedale Ltd, Liskeard, England
Printed in Hong Kong through Bookbuilders Ltd

Photographs and Line illustrations © *Paradise Press 1984*
Cover Photo: Angolan Peach-faced Lovebird

Contents

Introduction

The keeping and breeding of lovebirds has become increasingly popular over recent years, being reflected in the large range of mutations and color forms, second only in number to those of the budgerigar. The natural distribution of this genus of small, square-tailed, parrots ranges across much of the African continent and some off-shore islands. In some areas they reach plague proportions and huge numbers, perhaps thirty thousand birds, are destroyed annually in these regions.

Nine separate species are recognized by most taxonomists. One species is virtually unknown both in the wild and collections while others, such as the Red-faced, present a breeding challenge even for the experienced aviculturist. The Peach-faced Lovebird is currently the most popular member of the group and, usually being ready to nest, forms an ideal introduction to the group for the novice lovebird breeder.

Lovebirds in Australia

While most interest has been focussed on lovebirds as aviary subjects, 'Peachies' are often kept as pets in Australia. They become very tame and prove great characters, although not talented talkers, if obtained straight from the nest or when partially hand-reared. Many Australian breeders keep their birds in small colonies, apparently without severe outbreaks of fighting. Elsewhere, lovebirds are generally housed in pairs.

For those who wish to start colony breeding, there are various precautions which should be taken to reduce the risk of fighting, well in advance of the breeding season when squabbling is especially likely to break out. All birds should be introduced to the aviary at the same time, and any unpaired individuals subsequently removed. A minimum number of two nest-boxes per pair will need to be provided, and fixed at the same height, so that there is no risk of possible squabbling for the highest nesting site. The birds must never be overcrowded.

Purchasing Lovebirds

Healthy lovebirds look alert, and move readily when approached. The feathering around the vent should be clean, and the eyes free from any signs of discharge. Their plumage may be somewhat ragged, however,

3

especially in the case of imported birds. Lovebirds also have a tendency to pluck their feathers, giving a bald appearance, typically on the breast and neck, or top of the head; in the latter case another bird is likely to be the culprit. Youngsters may be plucked in the nest by their parents but, given time, these feathers will regrow satisfactorily.

Lovebirds can be caught from a stock cage by hand but, in an aviary, a net which is well-padded around the rim will be essential. A thin pair of gloves is also advisable because these birds can bite quite painfully. For a close examination, the head should be restrained *very gently* between the first two fingers of the hand, with the bird's back resting in the palm. It is then possible to feel the chest which should be plump, with no hollows either side of the breastbone. These hollows indicate weight-loss, described as 'going-light', and have various possible causes.

Acclimatization and Hardiness

Imported birds should not be put into an aviary when the weather is liable to turn cold, but must be kept in heated quarters. They can then be left out throughout the warmer months, but may need to be brought in again for the following winter; after this they should be able to winter outdoors successfully. Nest-boxes must always be provided for the birds to roost in throughout the year. Home-bred stock from an outdoor aviary can be moved safely to another flight at any time of the year, and so is recommended. Some of the less common species, however, such as the Red-faced, cannot really be considered fully hardy in North American and European climates.

A Note on Nomenclature

With the sudden explosion of color mutations and forms, considerable confusion and comment have arisen concerning the nomenclature for these different colors. As an example, Henning Jacobsen carried out a survey of the terms currently used in Britain during 1980, and counted over one hundred and ten different descriptions. Similar confusion exists on the European mainland, with over eighty terms being used by approximately forty-two German breeders, to describe their stock in advertisements.

There is an overwhelming need for rationalisation if people are not to be put off these birds when faced with such a confusing range of names for the various colors. In the text that follows, I have tried to employ the most widely-used terms such as Pastel Blue, while listing alternatives; although I accept that not all could be considered ideal. In this case the color of the bird is greenish, not pastel-blue which is, therefore, a misnomer for descriptive purposes.

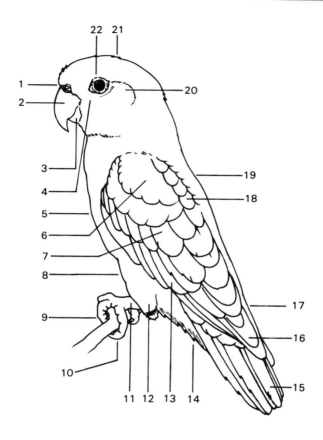

DESCRIPTIVE FEATURES OF A LOVEBIRD

1 Cere
2 Upper mandible
3 Lower mandible
4 Lores
5 Breast
6 Lesser wing coverts
7 Secondary coverts
8 Abdomen
9 Toes
10 Claw
11 Shank

12 Thigh
13 Secondaries
14 Under tail coverts
15 Central tail feathers
16 Primaries
17 Rump
18 Scapulars
19 Mantle
20 Ear coverts
21 Occiput (crown)
22 Periophthalmic (eye) ring

1. Accommodation

Lovebirds do not require elaborate accommodation, a simple aviary comprised of shelter and flight units being sufficient to meet their needs. A small block of such aviaries can be easily constructed, but both faces of adjoining flights must be wired over so the birds cannot bite their neighbors' feet through the mesh. It is always advisable to check whether any planning restrictions apply in a given location, before commencing building operations.

The Flight

Wired panels, which simply need to be assembled, can be obtained from many of the firms advertising in avicultural magazines, such as *Cage and Aviary Birds* or *Bird World*. These provide a useful short-cut to building an aviary, especially if they are weather-proofed with a suitable preservative. A jointed framework, built to one's own requirements, can also be made without too much difficulty. A practical size for a flight for a pair of lovebirds is 2·7 m. (9 ft) long, 0·9 m. (3 ft) wide and 1·8 m. (6 ft) in height.

All timber used for the flight should be at least 3·75 cm. (1½ in.) square. It can be treated with creosote before being assembled into frames, and this will then be quite safe, providing the woodwork is allowed to dry thoroughly over several weeks, before the birds are released into the aviary.

The mesh used to cover the flight panels can be 19 gauge (G) but preferably should be stouter 16 G. The dimensions of the netting are important because a 2·5 cm. (1 in.) square mesh will allow the entry of mice, other rodents and even snakes into the aviary. These creatures will disturb the birds even if they do not harm them directly. Therefore, a better size to use is 2·5 × 1·25 cm. (1 × ½ in.) netting.

The wire itself should be attached, using netting staples, to the planed inner surfaces of the jointed frame, as this will subsequently prevent the birds whittling the woodwork away. Any exposed and potentially dangerous ends of wire must be cut back as far as possible and covered with thin battens, which may need to be replaced at intervals if destroyed.

Shelter

A dry, draft-proof shelter, attached to the flight, will also be necessary, and must be well-lit to encourage the birds to roost therein when the weather is bad. A door, leading from the shelter into the flight, should be included in the design, along with an entrance hole located near the roof for the birds. Their entry can be facilitated by providing a simple landing platform either side of the entrance. Feeding the birds inside the shelter is to be recommended, and serves to keep their food dry. A shelter approximately 0·9 m. (3 ft) square is an ideal complement to the flight previously suggested.

Foundations

The whole structure should be mounted on a firm base, constructed using blocks or bricks sunk into the ground around the perimeter. Apart from providing additional stability, with the aviary bolted to its base, this

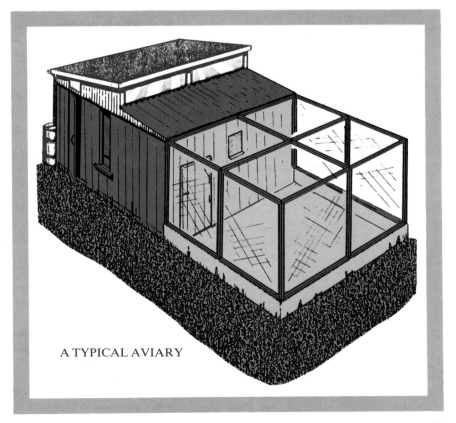

A TYPICAL AVIARY

should also serve to keep out rodents and foxes which might otherwise tunnel in, often with fatal consequences.

Ideally, the floor of the flight should be concrete, which is much easier than grass to clean satisfactorily, and should be sloped to allow for drainage in wet weather. The shelter will also require a solid floor.

Perches

These can be made in the shape of a 'T' and fixed in the floor, or suspended by means of wire loops which attach firmly to the aviary framework. Perches should always run across the flight, rather than down its length. Wood used for perches should not have been sprayed with chemicals, as is the case with many fruit trees. In addition, branches cut from some trees, such as yew, lilac and laburnum may prove poisonous to the birds, and should be avoided. As an additional precaution, all branches used should be washed down before the birds have access to them.

Roofing

The roof of the flight for perhaps 0·9 m. (3 ft) nearest to the shelter and a similar distance on the sides, should be covered with translucent plastic sheeting. This will enable the birds to sit outside with some degree of protection when the weather is bad.

The shelter can be conveniently roofed with marine plywood, all cracks being filled with a suitable water-proofing material and tarred over, before thick roofing felt is applied. This should overlap down the sides of the shelter for several inches. As a final precaution to ensure that the interior remains dry, guttering should be attached along the back of the sloping roof, to carry off rainwater, away from the aviary.

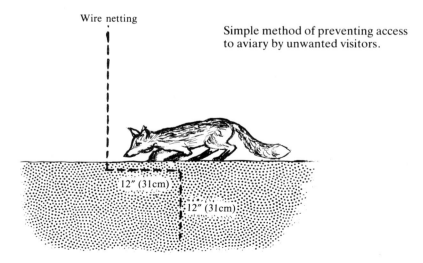

Wire netting

Simple method of preventing access to aviary by unwanted visitors.

12″ (31cm)

12″ (31cm)

8

2. Feeding

Lovebirds are not difficult birds to feed, and they will thrive if given a mixture of seeds and some green-food daily. Plain canary-seed, millet of various types (especially panicum), and sunflower seed make up most mixtures, given in a ratio of approximately 3:2:1. Oats are sometimes used as a supplementary foodstuff, generally offered soaked during the breeding season. Seed should only be purchased from a reliable source, preferably in bags, and then stored in bins to keep it dry and away from rodents, whose excrement can transmit serious diseases, like salmonellosis, to the birds if it is allowed to contaminate the seed.

Soaked Seed

When seed is immersed in water, it is encouraged to sprout and the chemical changes, which would naturally accompany germination, take place thus altering its feeding value. Vitamin and protein levels increase, while the seed itself is also rendered more digestible. Therefore, soaked seed is commonly fed when there are chicks in the nest, and to birds recovering from illness. It can also be offered daily throughout the year, and contributes a useful variation to the diet.

The required quantity will need to be left to soak for a day in a warm environment, and then washed thoroughly in a sieve. Only small amounts should be prepared at any one time, because molds soon develop on such seed, and that remaining uneaten must be discarded at the end of the day. Feeding containers, separate from those used for dry seed, are necessary. Most seeds can be prepared in this way and, while millet sprays are a traditional favorite, mung beans are now being used much more widely, given either soaked or sprouted. These can be obtained either from specialist seed-merchants or health-food stores.

Green-food

Greenstuff, such as fresh-cut lettuce, chickweed or spinach beet is popular with most lovebirds. Spinach has the additional advantage that, when planted in a garden, a supply is generally available throughout the year, even during the winter. Seeding grasses of various types, including cultivated cereal seeds such as millet, are greedily taken by the vast majority of birds. Sweet apple and carrot also prove acceptable to some individuals.

Whenever gathering fresh foods for the birds, care should be taken to ensure that it has not been fouled by other animals, or contaminated by chemical sprays. Roadside verges are especially hazardous as collecting areas because, apart from the risk of spraying, the lead levels of the vegetation are generally higher as a result of vehicle fumes. This chemical can accumulate in the body until toxic levels are reached.

Grit and Cuttlefish

Both are important sources of essential minerals, with grit serving also to assist with the digestion of food, and they should always be available to the birds. Cuttlefish bone is a major source of calcium, required particularly during the breeding season for sound egg-shells and a healthy skeletal structure in the chicks. These bones are often found washed up on beaches, especially at certain times of the year. Providing they are not contaminated with tar, cuttlebones can be used safely, after being thoroughly cleaned, soaked in water which is changed daily for about a week, and then finally washed thoroughly before being allowed to dry.

Additional Food Supplements

A range of high-protein softbill-type mixes are now available and will be valuable, especially during the breeding season, if the birds will take this food. Various tonics can also be beneficial, providing they are used as directed. Harmful side-effects may well result from the overuse of such products.

The Yellow mutation of the Fischer's Lovebird (*see text on page 41*).

3. Breeding

There are various systems being used for breeding lovebirds, depending on the species concerned and the region of the world. The requirements of the Red-faced, for example, are relatively specialised; success using just a plain nest-box is unlikely with this species.

Sexing

The first major problem to be overcome with species which are not sexually dimorphic is to select actual pairs. Purchasing several birds of the chosen species, and keeping them as a group, at least until they pair off, offers a partial solution. Pairs should roost together, so smearing the entrance hole of a box with lipstick will serve to identify the birds concerned – some of the marker being transferred to their plumage as they move in and out. However, this system is not always practical, especially with the rarer and more expensive mutations. Surgical or laparotomy sexing offers a direct method of viewing the sex organs of the birds, and would appear to be feasible for lovebirds from the age of four months onwards. After the bird has been anesthetized the probe is inserted through a small incision in the flank. Although recovery in the majority of cases is uneventful, there is always a possibility of fatalities with this method. Other laboratory techniques for sexing are being studied, and may well supersede surgical sexing over the course of the next few years.

Before surgical sexing was available, fanciers looked for other characteristics to sex their birds. The physical appearance may give a clue, as hens often appear to have flatter heads, but this is not a reliable method of recognizing pairs. The pelvic bone test has a factual basis because, when hens are about to lay, the gap between their pelvic bones which, with care, can be felt as two bony prominences in front of the vent, is enlarged. This difference is not seen in cocks, young birds or hens out of breeding condition, so the application of the test is rather limited.

The behavior of the lovebirds prior to breeding can be significant. These birds belong to one of the few genera of psittacines which build a nest, and this activity is carried out almost exclusively by the female. Thus, if both lovebirds carry nesting material, and then a large number of clear eggs are laid, it is likely that the 'pair' is comprised of two hens. Conversely, lack of interest in breeding, and no eggs, indicates that the birds may well prove to be cocks.

Nest-boxes

Lovebirds should always have access to a nest-box for roosting purposes throughout the year, but it is preferable to restrict the breeding season to the warmer months. Some species, such as the Peach-faced, will breed all the year round when given the opportunity, but more problems and fewer chicks are likely to result if the birds are breeding outdoors during winter. However, pairs of Madagascar Lovebirds often choose to nest at this time and, for this reason, should be kept in a heated bird-room to maximize their chances of breeding successfully.

As a general rule, nest-boxes should be relatively small and compact, about 17·5 cm. (7 in.) square and 22·5 cm. (9 in.) high, with an entrance hole not exceeding 5 cm. (2 in.) in diameter. The roof of the structure should be hinged for inspection purposes, while a perch located just below the entrance will give the lovebirds easy access to the nesting site. The more specialized requirements of the rare Red-faced Lovebird are discussed later in the species section.

The nest-box is best located in the outside flight, under cover where it will be protected from the excesses of the weather, and yet where the humidity will be higher than in the aviary shelter. Lovebirds, especially members of the White eye-ringed group, have a reputation for producing a significant proportion of chicks which do not hatch, and low humidity is one factor which may be involved in such failures.

It is useful to have two identical nest-boxes for each pair, so that a clean box can be provided for breeding purposes at the appropriate time of year. The other box should be removed and thoroughly cleaned. This will ensure that the hen lays in a nest-box which is free from red mite which can soon build up in large numbers when the nest is occupied permanently. They can severely handicap the development of the chicks, by sucking their blood, and may lead to an increased incidence of feather-plucking, by virtue of the irritation which they can cause.

Nesting Material

The type and quantity of nesting material required depends somewhat on the species of lovebird. Abyssinians, at one extreme, only construct a simple pad, often largely comprised of the hen's breast feathers, whereas Masked Lovebirds will build a more elaborate structure, which may have a distinct dome in a large nest-box. Therefore, some breeders prefer to have a hinged door at the front of the box to give them better access to the nest, but there is an increased risk of eggs and chicks falling out – unless the door is opened very carefully.

12

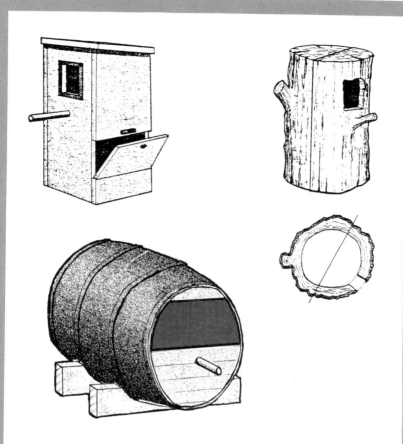

LOVEBIRD NEST-BOXES

A typical design is shown on the top left, with a variation of this on the right. The barrel and long-box have been used successfully for Red-faced Lovebirds which have more specialized feeding requirements.

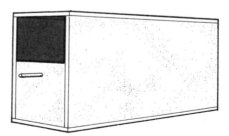

Branches of non-poisonous deciduous trees, such as elder and hazel, should be provided, preferably standing in water in a narrow-necked vessel such as a bottle. The lovebirds will then cut their nesting material and the hen can construct her nest with fresh leaves, stems and bark which should help to increase the humidity in the nestbox. Peach-faced Lovebirds, and possibly Swindern's, carry material tucked in amongst the feathers of the back and rump, whereas White eye-ringed birds transfer it to the nest in their beaks.

The Breeding Period

Prior to laying, the hen will take more cuttlefish bone, which must be freely available, and her droppings often become larger. Eggs are usually produced every other day, and the clutch may vary in size from one to eight eggs, although between four and six is usual. The hen incubates alone, but the cock may join his mate in the nest for periods and feed her during this time.

The incubation period is approximately twenty-three days for all species, but this is somewhat variable, depending partly on when incubation actually began in earnest. Many hens do not start sitting until they have laid two or three eggs. This in turn ensures that the chicks are of a more even age when they hatch, and thus improves their chances of survival. If the weather is cold, it is likely that the incubation period will be prolonged slightly.

Most lovebird species cannot be housed together in numbers but the Red-faced (*Agapornis pullaria*) is an exception.

The very popular Peach-faced
Lovebird (*Agapornis roseicollis catumbella*) —
the Angolan form.

The youngsters generally fledge when about six weeks old but are still fed, largely by the cock, for a short time until they are eating independently. They should then be removed to separate accommodation because lovebirds, in spite of their name, can be very vicious towards each other. If the hen is preparing to lay another round of eggs, she will almost certainly attack, and may even kill, her earlier youngsters if they are allowed to remain in the same quarters.

The provision of an additional nest-box at this time may help to overcome the problem temporarily, so that the youngsters can roost elsewhere than in the original nesting site. Fighting is especially likely to occur if the birds are being bred in the confines of a cage.

Problems During the Breeding Season

Some potential problems, such as egg-binding and French Molt, are discussed later. Failure of eggs to hatch is a relatively common problem, which can occur for two reasons, either they were not fertilised or the embryos died in the shell. In the latter instance, the egg appears opaque, rather than relatively clear, when viewed in a good light. The degree of humidity may have been at fault, or mineral deficiencies could be responsible. Indeed, any shortcomings in the diet will be emphasised when the birds are breeding, so that poor hatching, sickly chicks and feather-plucking may result from poor nutrition.

As suggested previously, a diet of seed alone is deficient in various respects, especially with regard to protein, therefore it is preferable to offer supplementary foods throughout the year, and simply increase the quantities when chicks are in the nest. Bread-and-milk, for example, is a valuable supplement, providing essential amino acids which are deficient in the protein of seeds. These can be passed on, via the protein contained in the egg, and then directly to the developing birds, thus leading to improved breeding results overall. However, all perishable foodstuffs must be removed before they can turn sour.

On occasions, it may be necessary to foster out chicks and, fortunately, the vast majority of pairs will readily accept this additional burden, providing their chicks are of a compatible age. Eggs can also be moved satisfactorily, as long as there is no large discrepancy in the dates of laying, otherwise the youngest chicks, even if they hatch, are unlikely to survive when competing with much older nest-mates.

4. Color Breeding

Although mutations are now established in various species of lovebird, their mode of inheritance will fit into one of the four simple groupings based on the work of the pioneering geneticist Gregor Mendel. Structures referred to as genes control all features of an individual, including color, and occur on chromosomes. In turn, these chromosomes are paired, so that there are two genes for each characteristic, located on opposing chromosomes.

Autosomal recessive mutations

As the number of offspring produced increases, so the chances of a mutant occurring are correspondingly higher. In the majority of cases, however, the natural coloration remains dominant, and the mutation is thus referred to as a recessive. If only one member of a pair of genes becomes mutated, in this example for Pastel Blue, then the bird will still appear like a normal green Peach-faced, but carry the Pastel Blue gene in its genetic make-up. This mutant gene can later be expressed if the lovebird is paired with a similar 'split' or another Pastel Blue. There are in fact five possible basic pairings for mutations of this type:–

1. Pastel Blue × Green → 100% Green/Pastel Blue.
2. Pastel Blue × Green/Pastel Blue → 50% Pastel Blue + 50% Green/Pastel Blue.
3. Pastel Blue × Pastel Blue → 100% Pastel Blue.
4. Green/Pastel Blue × Green → 50% Green/Pastel Blue + 50% Green.
5. Green/Pastel Blue × Green/Pastel Blue → 50% Green/Pastel Blue + 25% Pastel Blue + 25% Green.

The oblique line indicates that the bird is split for the second color (or character), with the dominant feature preceding it. Such birds, with differing genes, are also referred to as heterozygous, while those which are pure may be called homozygous.

Sex-linked recessive mutations

Such mutations are confined exclusively to the pair of sex chromosomes,

A Gray Peach-faced lovebird

A Blue Peach-faced lovebird chick

which can be distinguished between the sexes; while the remaining chromosomes are known collectively as autosomes. In the case of the cock, both members of the pair of sex chromosomes are of the same length, whereas hens have one of these (often denoted as 'Y') shorter than the other (known as 'Z' or 'X'). Therefore, it is not possible for a hen to be split for a mutation which occurs on the unpaired part of the chromosome, because there is no corresponding portion for a gene on the opposing chromosome to be present, and thus suppress it. Peach-faced hens must be either Lutino or Green and, unlike cocks, they cannot be Green/Lutino. Expected results for such pairings are:

1. Green cock × Lutino hen → 50% Green/Lutino cocks + 50% Green hens.
2. Green/Lutino cock × Green hen → 25% Green cocks + 25% Green/Lutino cocks + 25% Green hens + 25% Lutino hens.
3. Green/Lutino cock × Lutino hen → 25% Green/Lutino cocks + 25% Lutino cocks + 25% Green hens + 25% Lutino hens.
4. Lutino cock × Green hen → 50% Green/Lutino cocks + 50% Lutino hens.
5. Lutino cock × Lutino hen → 50% Lutino cocks + 50% Lutino hens.

In individual cases, the chicks produced will probably not conform to the expected results, simply because these are based on expectancies from a large number of pairings. As more chicks are produced from an individual pair, the closer expected, and actual, results will correlate assuming, of course, that the genotypes for the birds are accurately known. It cannot be assumed, for example, that a supposedly split Lutino cock does not, in fact carry the mutant gene if no Lutino offspring emerge in just one nest of chicks. The presence of a single Lutino chick will, however, be sufficient to confirm that its father is heterozygous, if its mother is Green.

Dominant mutations

There is, however, one recognized Peach-faced mutation which is dominant to Green; thus, for the Pied, a reverse situation to the autosomal recessive mutation exists. In this case, the mutant birds are known as single or double factor (s.f. and d.f. respectively), depending whether one or both genes are affected. The possible Pied pairings are shown below:–

1. Pied (s.f.) × Green → 50% Pied (s.f.) + 50% Green.
2. Pied (d.f.) × Green → 100% Pied (s.f.).
3. Pied (s.f.) × Pied (s.f.) → 50% Pied (s.f.) + 25% Pied (d.f.) + 25% Green.
4. Pied (s.f.) × Pied (d.f.) → 50% Pied (s.f.) + 50% Pied (d.f.).
5. Pied (d.f.) × Pied (d.f.) → 100% Pied (d.f.).

Once again, it is not possible to distinguish between the single and double factor birds by visual means. If Greens result from the pairing of a Pied with a Green, however, then the former must be a single factor bird.

Incomplete dominant mutation

This mutation has the effect of modifying the depth of color, rather than the color itself. It can be recognized as an incomplete dominant mutation, because it is possible to distinguish between single and double-factor birds on grounds of their coloration, whereas this is impossible in the case of the preceding type of mutation. For Green Peach-faced, therefore, the expected results of the various pairings are:–

1. Olive (d.f.) × Olive (d.f.) → 100% Olive (d.f.).
2. Olive (d.f.) × Dark Green (s.f.) → 50% Olive (d.f.) + 50% Dark Green (s.f.).
3. Olive (d.f.) × Green (n.f.) → 100% Dark Green (s.f.)
4. Dark Green (s.f.) × Dark Green (s.f.) → 50% Dark Green (s.f.) + 25% Green + 25% Olive (d.f.)
5. Dark Green (s.f.) × Green (n.f.) → 50% Dark Green (s.f.) + 50% Green (n.f.)

   (n.f. = no dark factor present)

It has been possible to transfer the dark factor mutation to Pastel Blue birds, with the corresponding terms shown below:–

Green	No dark factor	Pastel Blue
Dark Green	One dark factor	Dark factor Pastel Blue
Olive Green	Two dark factors	Slate

Calculations for offspring expected from any pairing

It is possible to calculate the expected results from any pair of lovebirds simply by breaking down the genetic characteristics of the parents, and arranging these in the form of a square, at right angles to each other. The mating of a Pied with a Pastel Blue is given below as an example. The Pied's genetic make-up is abbreviated to PPBB, being dominant so that it is written in capitals, distinguishing it from the Pastel Blue which is recessive in character, and thus referred to as ppbb. This yields offspring which are all Pied (s.f.)/Pastel Blue (PpBb). When such birds are paired together, the following results can be expected though, again, it is not possible to distinguish between single and double factor birds, or split Pastel Blue individuals, without trial pairings.

PpBb Parent \\ Gametes				
PpBb Parent	**PB**	**Pb**	**pB**	**pb**
Gametes **PB**	PPBB Pied (d.f.)	PPBb Pied (d.f.)/ Pastel Blue	PpBB Pied (s.f.)	PpBb Pied (s.f.)/ Pastel Blue
Pb	PPbB Pied (d.f.)/ Pastel Blue	PPbb Pastel Blue Pied (d.f.)	PpbB Pied (s.f.)/ Pastel Blue	Ppbb Pastel Blue Pied (s.f.)
pB	pPBB Pied (s.f.)	pPBb Pied (s.f.)/ Pastel Blue	ppBB Green	ppBb Green/Pastel Blue
pb	pPBb Pied (s.f.)/ Pastel Blue	pPbb Pastel Blue Pied (s.f.)	ppbB Green/Pastel Blue	ppbb Pastel Blue

5. The Lovebird Species

Classification

The purpose of classification is to divide the entire animal kingdom into a series of groups (called ranks) based on the similarities of features found within animals. The higher the group the more general its characteristics. Thus, the highest rank is that of Kingdom, embracing all living forms and these are divided into many phyla each containing many members, all of which share common features. Phyla are divided into classes, these into orders, and so on until one reaches the individual animal or species, by which time the animals resemble each other in all but the very smallest of detail.

Over the years, and with the advances in knowledge of the various animals, it becomes necessary to continually revise the classification, especially of the lower ranks. For this reason, you will see differences in classifications given by various authors which represent the extent of information on that bird or group of birds at that point in time. In order to overcome possible confusion in the nomenclature of animals, it is internationally agreed that Latin be used for this purpose.

The classification used in this book is based on that proposed by Peters in *Checklist of Birds of the World* (1937). All birds belong to the class Aves with the order Psittaciformes embracing lovebirds as well as all other psittacines (parrot-like birds).

The lowest two ranks, the genus and the species, when used together, identify the members of a single interbreeding group or species. Within a species, there may be one or more races which differ sufficiently to warrant them being given the rank of sub-species and this is denoted by an extra name appearing after the species name. It is customary to write the scientific name in italics, or the genus if used by itself, but not for any rank above the genus. This latter group starts with a capital letter and the species name (the trivial) always commences with a lower case letter. The name which often appears after the specific name is that of the person who first classified it and, should the bird have changed from its original genus to a new one, then the person's name is placed in parenthesis. If the name is followed by a date, this signifies the date when first classified. Where a trivial name is repeated, this is called the nominate race and

The Yellow and Green Pied mutation of
the Peach-faced Lovebird is most attractive.

indicates it was the first of that species to be classified, it is therefore an example of the 'type' though, not necessarily, typical of the species.

The following example shows the classification of the Madagascar Lovebird	
Class:	Aves
Order:	Psittaciformes
Family:	Psittacidae
Sub-family:	Psittacinae
Genus:	*Agapornis* (Selby) 1836
Species:	*A. cana*
Sub-species:	*A. cana cana* (Gmelin) 1788
	A. cana ablectanea Bangs 1918

SEXUALLY DIMORPHIC GROUP

RED-FACED LOVEBIRD – *Agapornis pullaria* (Linnaeus) 1758

This species has a wide distribution in the wild, occurring especially in regions of grassland broken with trees. Large numbers may congregate to feed on cultivated crops; but smaller flocks, numbering up to about twenty individuals, are more commonly seen. They feed at ground level on grass seeds, and rarely allow a close approach, flying off at the slightest hint of danger. Their nesting habits are unusual, in that they excavate breeding chambers in the mounds of termites, located as high as 12 m. (40 ft) up in trees, and co-exist quite happily alongside the insects.

Although formerly common in Britain, Red-faced Lovebirds are currently very scarce, but two individuals can be seen in the excellent collection of parrots at Birdland, Bourton-on-the-Water in Gloucestershire. They are rather nervous birds by nature, and do not always prove easy to establish successfully. Elsewhere in Europe, they are still quite regularly available, and are being bred in increasing numbers.

Claims of breeding successes go back to the end of the last century, but some may well relate to the Peach-faced Lovebird. Arthur Prestwich was the first British breeder of this species, having repeated success during the mid-1950s, by providing barrels full of peat, positioned on their sides, which enabled the hen birds to excavate a breeding chamber.

Refinements of Prestwich's method have followed and, in a few collections, Red-faced Lovebirds are now being reared consistently. Herr Blome, in Germany, reared forty in the space of just five years, starting in 1974. He attributes this success to the provision of heating pads, which serve to maintain the temperature inside the box at 30°C. 85°F, once the chicks have hatched. Because of their nervous dispositions, Red-faced Lovebirds are slow to return to their nests when approached, so the young birds can soon become chilled.

24

Red-faced chicks have light reddish down at first and eventually fledge when about seven weeks old. Adult birds should always be offered a varied diet, particularly when they are breeding; one pair in a Danish collection were consuming large numbers of mealworms daily when rearing their two chicks.

Mutations

The only mutation reported in the case of the Red-faced Lovebird is a Lutino form, where green plumage is replaced by yellow, as melanin is lost; for this reason, the eyes are also red. It is extremely scarce at the time of writing, but examples are being kept by breeders in both Portugal and Switzerland, and such birds have been bred.

MADAGASCAR LOVEBIRD – *Agapornis cana* (Gmelin) 1788
Synonyms: Lavender-headed Lovebird; Gray-headed Lovebird

These lovebirds are common in Malagasy, frequenting the edges of woodland, and venturing out to feed on grass seeds and drying rice around areas of cultivation. Although generally shy and retiring by nature, exceptions are known. One young cock bird owned by Graham Thurlow delighted in having its head scratched regularly. Madagascar Lovebirds are only irregularly available, having been first imported to Britain during 1860, and never in large numbers. In recent years, hens have proved much harder to obtain than cocks, which has hampered breeding attempts.

Successful results have not been obtained consistently, partly because these lovebirds seem to prefer to nest during the winter months. For serious breeding attempts, therefore, pairs should be housed indoors, preferably in small flights. The nest-box should be located in a secluded position, by providing a suitable screen of translucent plastic around the appropriate region of the flight framework. Infertile clutches can be a problem – probably because the cock is reluctant to approach his dominant mate too closely.

Madagascar Lovebirds seem prone to breathing difficulties resulting from air-sac mites, which actually live in the airways. These parasites can be eliminated by means of a dichlorvos preparation, usually in the form of a strip more commonly used for killing flies, which is hung in the room where the birds are housed. However, unnecessary exposure to this potentially toxic chemical should be avoided.

Mutations

No mutation of this species has yet been recorded.

25

The Abyssinian or Black-winged
Lovebird cock (*Agapornis taranta*)

Madagascar Lovebird cock
(*Agapornis cana cana*)

ABYSSINIAN LOVEBIRD – *Agapornis taranta* (Stanley) 1814
Synonym: Black-winged Lovebird

Abyssinian Lovebirds are birds of the highlands, reflected by their larger size, and range up to altitudes of about 3000 m. (10,000 ft). There are often wide temperature variations in these regions, perhaps as much as 30°C 85°F between day and night-time readings; the lovebirds naturally use holes in trees as roosting sites, for protection against the bitter nights. When breeding, Abyssinian hens use little nesting material, apart from their own feathers and, in some cases, may completely denude their breasts for this purpose.

Abyssinian Lovebirds have never been very common in collections and, currently, cocks seem especially scarce. Chicks were first reared successfully in Germany during 1924, followed by other breedings in Britain and France. Young birds hatch with a coat of thin, white down, which is replaced by gray as they get older. Fledging normally occurs at the age of seven weeks. Figs often prove popular with these lovebirds, and sweet apple is also a favorite of some individuals. A few pairs may have two successive rounds of chicks, but this is the exception rather than the rule.

Mutations

A Cinnamon form has been reported, in which the flight feathers only are brown. The secondary flight feathers and underwing coverts remain black, with the body coloration overall slightly lighter than normal. A single bird of this type was imported by John Wood, of Ponderosa Bird Aviaries in about 1973, and subsequently passed to George Smith. It produced ten cocks when paired to a normal, but never any hens, and the mode of inheritance of the mutant was not discovered. However, the descendants of this bird are still present in some British aviaries, so there is a slim chance that the mutation may re-emerge in the future.

INTERMEDIATE GROUP

SWINDERN'S BLACK-COLLARED LOVEBIRD – *Agapornis swinderniana* (Kuhl) 1820
Synonyms: Liberian Lovebird; Swinderen's Lovebird

There are very few recorded observations of these lovebirds in the wild, and it is unlikely that any have reached Europe alive. They were named after the Dutchman Dr T. van Swinderen, but there was an error in the original spelling of their scientific name, which could not subsequently be corrected. Recent reports suggest that their range is much wider than previously thought, extending into Ghana. Birds belonging to the nominate race rarely descend from the tree tops, according to one ornithologist who has observed them in the wild. They are, therefore, very inconspicuous [so he told me] and probably more common than has been suspected.

Father Hutsebout attempted to keep some of these birds in Zaire, but found that they did not survive without figs. He made no attempt to wean them gradually on to other foods, but merely withdrew figs from their diet – which was courting disaster by suddenly confronting them with unfamiliar foodstuffs. Examination of the contents of the crops of shot specimens, has revealed that millet and even insects are taken by these birds. George Smith recounted to me his meeting with a man who lived in Nigeria, and who claimed to have an aviary of Swindern's Lovebirds thriving on a diet comprised largely of seed. It is possible that a few pairs may be imported in the not-too-distant future, and so enable aviculturists to add greatly to existing knowledge concerning this species. Having examined a large number of skins of the various subspecies, in my opinion, the beak of this bird, being relatively slender, more closely resembles that of a Hanging Parrot than any other lovebird.

Mutations

Not surprisingly, none is currently known.

PEACH-FACED LOVEBIRD – *Agapornis roseicollis* (Vieillot) 1817
Synonym: Rosy-faced Lovebird

Peach-faced Lovebirds were first identified as being a subspecies of the Red-faced, back in 1793, but were then recognized as being a different species in 1817. They occur in relatively arid areas, but rarely stray far from water. These birds will breed in a variety of sites, even taking over the nests of weavers such as the Sociable (*Philetairus socius*) and Mahali (*Plocepasser mahali*) species.

Hens are responsible for building the nest, cutting strips of wood about 10 cm (4 in.) in length, which are then bent in half and transferred to the feathers of the back and rump, to be carried to the chosen site. They can transfer six or so strips at a time in this way, but any which are dropped en route to the nest are not picked up later. Chicks hatch with a coat of rather dense, red down feathering which is replaced by gray down from the age of ten days onwards. Fledging occurs when the youngsters are about six weeks old.

Peach-faced Lovebirds are currently the most prolific and popular members of the genus, worldwide; they are still freely available in Australia, where imports of birds have been banned for several decades. This has been reflected in the number of color mutations and forms which are now being bred in ever-increasing numbers.

Mutations

1. Pastel Blue. (Illustrated above)
Synonyms: Par Blue; Sea Green; Blue

This mutation first appeared in the aviaries of a Dutchman, P. Habats back in 1963. Out of a nest of five chicks, there were two Pastel Blues, and another was produced from the next clutch of eggs. This mutation has now become the most widely-kept form in Europe, which is perhaps surprising, bearing in mind its recessive nature. On the European mainland, such birds are generally referred to as 'Blues', but the description is

30

definitely a misnomer, because they are, in fact, greenish-blue with a cream rather than white face. This is because some, but not all, of the reddish-yellow pigment has been eliminated.

Much interest has been generated by the appearance of a White-faced Blue. The first European breeders were Mallmann in Holland and Eyckerman in Belgium around 1977, while similar birds have also been produced in America. Mallmann's birds were obtained from Dark Green/ Pastel Blue stock, which was paired together. Such White-faces still have the faintest pinkish tinge which is most visible on the crown, while retaining a greenish suffusion on the head and wings.

Subsequent breeding results have now confirmed that the White-faced Blue is not a completely separate mutation from the Pastel Blue, because pairing the two forms together does not yield Green/Pastel Blue and White-faced Blue, as would be anticipated if this was in fact the case. It now appears that the White-faced form is simply a modification of the Pastel Blue mutation, known technically as an allele.

Japanese Golden Cherry (*left*),
American Pied Silver Cherry (*center*),
and Pied Golden Cherry mutations of
the Peach-faced Lovebird.

2. Yellow Forms of the Peach-faced

The first reported yellow mutation of the Peach-faced Lovebird came from Japan where, in 1954, Mr Iwata bred a type which subsequently became known rather – fancifully – as the 'Cherryhead' or 'Golden Cherry'. This mutation is thus named after its reddish face, which contrasts with the yellowish body and blue rump. These Japanese birds were introduced to Europe from the late 1960s onwards, with Dr Burkard being one of the first breeders to obtain them. However, the stock did not appear very strong, and even today, these birds are not among the most prolific of the mutants now being bred, and remain relatively expensive.

A pair of the Japanese Cherryheads were sent to America, and a strain of this color has been developed. Some breeders refer to a darker form as the American Golden Cherryhead, but it would not now appear to be a separate mutation. Pairing light and dark birds together does not yield green offspring, which suggests that the difference simply results from another allele.

Two separate yellow Peach-faced mutations have been recorded from Australia. One type is confusingly called 'Cinnamon' but is, in fact, deep yellow in color with a slight greenish tinge to the body. These birds have sky-blue rumps, and retain a reddish face and tail markings. The mode of inheritance differs from that of the Golden Cherryhead and chicks hatch with red eyes, which then become progressively darker to resemble those of the latter color variety. A more attractive mutation, simply called 'Yellow' (or 'Buttercup') in Australia, has black eyes, but otherwise strongly resembles Lutinos in the depth and purity of color. It can be recognized, however, because it lacks the circular, deeper red patch of feathering present on the crown of the Lutino, and its rump has a turquoise-green cast.

The Lutino itself originated in America, being developed in California, initially by Mrs Schertzer in San Diego during 1970. In this case, the eyes are red, and the rump is white rather than blue. With no melanin present in these birds, they are an even shade of yellow, with no hint of green suffusion in the plumage. A separate Lutino strain has occurred in Australia, but birds of this type remain scarce.

3. Pied

This mutation may have appeared in California as early as the 1930s, according to Jim Hayward; but it came to prominence during the 1960s. It may have been that these early individuals had a metabolic malfunction which gave them pied markings, and that it was not a genetic trait. The distribution of pied markings is very variable, and cannot be predicted accurately for a given pair of birds; but, at present, the trend is towards selecting individuals which show predominantly ground color, such as

32

yellow rather than green in this case. The pied factor has been combined with other mutations, as mentioned later.

4. The Dark factor

Olive Peach-faced Lovebirds (with two dark factors) were first bred in Australia by Alan Hollingsworth in Victoria during 1968. This now appears to be the most widespread mutation there, which is perhaps not surprising in view of its mode of inheritance. The overall body color, apart from the face, is darkened, so the rump in such birds is bluish-gray, and the flight feathers black. Dark Greens, possessing a single dark factor, are intermediate in coloration between the Olive and normal Green in these respects.

5. Cinnamon

Another American mutation, such birds have a brownish tinge to their plumage and are slightly paler than normal, although the pink facial coloration is unaffected. It is not a very striking mutation.

6. Other Mutations

Several other mutations of the Peach-faced are known, but information on them is not yet complete. Fallows were developed in Germany commencing in 1976, with a separate strain now recognised in East Germany. The chick initially produced had red eyes, with yellowish-green body coloration; the feet were pink rather than gray as is the case with the Cherryhead. Bodo Ochs has been instrumental in establishing the mutation there, but feels that females are weak at present. He has also developed a gray mutation in his aviaries, starting from a single youngster bred in 1978. Birds of this type are grayer in color than Pastel Blues, and also have paler masks. I was told of a Gray Peach-faced in Australia during 1980, but was unable to obtain any definite information about it. A violet factor, similar to that in Budgerigars, has been reported from Switzerland, where it was first bred in a colony aviary during 1976. It was a deep, dark cobalt color with a violet rump.

Color Combinations of the Peach-faced Mutations

A wide array of possible color combinations can now be bred, using these basic mutations, the majority of which are outlined briefly below.

Peach-faced Lovebirds showing varying degrees of red in areas of green plumage are relatively common, but this feature may only be transitory, resulting from a metabolic, and not a genetic, defect. A genuine Red Peach-faced may yet emerge, however. The most recent development in the field of Peach-faced mutations, taking place in America, is the breeding of birds with yellow rather than the normal pink facial coloration. A mutation known as the Gray-wing has also been reported in America, and is apparently lime green in color.

Pairing Pastel Blue Peach-faced with Cherryheads gives rise, in the second generation, to the so-called 'Silver Cherry' form. This is not white, as would be expected if a genuine blue mutant was used in the first instance. Such birds have a very pale pink face, somewhat darker on the crown, and pale yellowish-white plumage with a bluish tinge. This form is known as 'Ivory' in Australia, when the Yellow is used instead of the Cherryhead.

Using a Lutino, instead of the Cherryhead, gives rise to the Cream Lutino. Individuals of this type are red-eyed, with a lemon body-color. The Lutino is of course a sex-linked mutation so, in this case, the initial pairing should be made using a Lutino cock. All hens from this pairing

Cream-Albino (*right*) and American Pied Silver Cherry Peach-faced lovebirds.

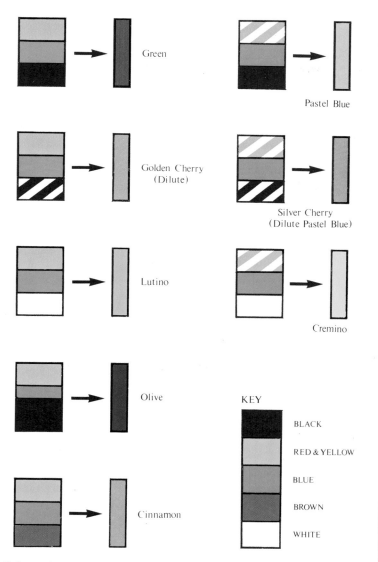

Green

Pastel Blue

Golden Cherry
(Dilute)

Silver Cherry
(Dilute Pastel Blue)

Lutino

Cremino

Olive

KEY

BLACK

RED & YELLOW

BLUE

BROWN

WHITE

Cinnamon

Schematic representation to show how changes in pigment distribution influence color in lovebirds using the Peach-faced as an example. Cross-hatching indicates reduction in pigment intensity.

will be lutino in color and the cocks green. Both will be split for Pastel Blue and Cream Lutino, and the cocks additionally for Lutino. Mating the corresponding offspring, preferably using two pairs at the outset to avoid in-breeding, will then yield Cream Lutinos of both sexes.

Pied Pastel Blues can be produced, with the resulting birds being pale yellow and sea green, rather than white and blue, since some psittacin remains. The white-faced form also gives rise to birds of this type.

The Dark factors can be introduced to Pastel Blue birds, as outlined earlier, to emerge as usual in the second generation offspring. Dark Pastel Blues have a cobalt rump; Slates, with two dark factors, possess a mauve rump. Probably, this cross was first achieved in Switzerland, whereas in Britain, Jack Horridge was amongst the first breeders of Slates in the early 1980s.

Dark factor Pieds have also been bred, and such birds can be very attractive, with the contrast between the olive and yellow markings. In the case of the Australian Yellow, dark factor birds of this type are known as Mustards and Olive Yellows respectively. Doubtless, as Cinnamons become more widely-available, they will be combined regularly with the other mutations, giving rise to Cinnamon Pieds and Pastel Blues at the outset.

Color combination required	Initial pairing (F_1)	Final pairing (F_2)
Silver Cherry	Pastel Blue x Cherryhead	Pair offspring together
Cream Lutino	Lutino cock x Pastel Blue hen	Pair offspring together
Pied Pastel Blue	Pied x Pastel Blue	Pair resulting normal pieds together, or to Pastel Blues
Dark Factor Pastel Blues (Also applies to Yellows)	Olive x Pastel Blue	Pair offspring together to produce both single factor and double dark factor Pastel Blues
Dark Factor Pieds	Olive x Pied	Gives Pied Dark Green which, if paired with Olives, will yield Pied Olives. Same effect can be achieved pairing the Pied Dark Green together

Table to show possible ways of producing various color combinations from the basic mutations. In-breeding should be avoided if at all possible when building up strains of such birds. The genotypes of all the birds involved can be worked out, using the Punnett Square system.

WHITE EYE-RINGED GROUP

Masked Lovebird – *Agapornis personata* (Reichenow) 1887
Synonym: Black-masked Lovebird; Yellow-collared Lovebird

The four remaining members of the genus are classified as related subspecies by some taxonomists, with the Masked being accorded the status of being the nominate race. They do have various features in common and, although their plumage differs in color, all possess the characteristic area of bare, white skin encircling the eyes: Because of this they are often referred to as the White eye-ringed group. Natural hybridization between these lovebirds would appear to be uncommon, however, but it has been recorded.

Populations are usually isolated, and yet these White eye-ring Lovebirds may range relatively close to each other, Fischer's and Masked, for example, occur within 65 km. (40 miles) of each other at one point, but do not come into direct contact, probably because the intervening vegetation is unsuitable for their feeding requirements. However, these lovebirds are found alongside each other in the region of Tanga, in north-east Tanzania, where populations have grown up following the release of captive birds during the 1920s.

The first breeding success with the Masked was achieved by K. Painter, of Ohio, USA in 1926, who obtained the first three birds seen during the previous year. Masked Lovebirds then became available to aviculturists generally from 1927 onwards, and European successes soon followed. Today, these lovebirds are generally available, but do not usually prove as prolific as the Peach-faced. Stock in Australia is expensive, as no imports are permitted. When breeding, Masked Lovebirds build nests which are much more bulky than those of species mentioned previously. The nest is added to throughout the breeding cycle, and a distinctly woven structure is produced. Like other members of the group, young Masked Lovebirds hatch covered in red down, and fledge when about six weeks old.

Mutations

1. Blue Masked

The Blue Masked mutation originated from an individual, caught in the wild, which reached England during 1927. Another strain was developed in California, five years later, from imported 'split' birds, and this unrelated blood was to help the British line. In birds of this type, the beak is pale pink, and not bright red as in other corresponding blue psittacine mutations, such as the Ring-necked Parrakeet (*Psittacula krameri*). A red-beaked variant of the Blue Masked has, however, recently been recorded from a Belgian collection, but this is thought to be an acquired change, and not a genuine mutation.

These mutant lovebirds still command quite a high price. Dennis Allan, who has specialised in breeding Blue Masked for some years in Yorkshire, England, states that cocks of this mutation are less vigorous than hens, with the highest losses occurring in birds molting out when between five and eight months old.

2. Yellow forms of the Masked Lovebird

The Yellow Masked originated in America in about 1935, and is a dilute form of the normal. An apparently distinct Danish Yellow mutant occurred in the aviary of a Mr Neiles, and came to the attention of Poul Frandsen during 1964. He then obtained the original hen and, from this, a number of yellow offspring have since been developed. There can be a considerable variation in the color of these birds, with some resembling the Yellow Masked while others are buttercup-yellow with white primaries, yet retaining the dark face. The size of the Danish mutant birds is small, at present, but this can be overcome by outcrossings using normals.

A rare White example of
the Masked Lovebird, bred in Denmark.

The Masked Lovebird (*Agapornis personata*)
is an ideal variety for the beginner.

3. White Masked

A single pure-white individual has been bred, again in Denmark, by Poul Frandsen. It appeared in 1973, in a nest with three Blue Masked chicks, and its Blue father had a few white feathers. Apparently, this bird bred for five years, and sired more than twenty chicks but, even when paired with two of its daughters which should have been split for white, no white chicks were forthcoming. The likely reason for this is that the lack of color was not a characteristic caused by genes, but resulted from metabolic defect.

4. Other Masked mutations

Reports of Pastel Blues, which may have had a hybrid ancestry in Japan, bred in Denmark during 1973, and of Cinnamons, have been recorded. Henning Jacobsen has also informed me of scalloping seen on both 'white' and yellow birds, at a Danish show early in 1981, resembling the opaline pattern well-recognized in budgerigars, but gray rather than black. Some Masked Lovebirds also have more orange on their breasts than others, but this cannot be classed as a significant mutation. An attractive but hybrid Lutino form has been developed in Holland.

COMMONEST MASKED MUTATIONS				
Mutation	**Synonyms**	**Origin**	**Mode of inheritance**	**Reason for color change**
Blue	—	Wild-caught	Autosomal recessive	Loss of psittacin
Yellow	Dilute	USA	Autosomal recessive	Partial loss of melanin
Danish Yellow	—	Denmark	Autosomal recessive	Increased loss of melanin over the above mutation

Color Combinations of the Masked Mutations

Only the incorrectly-named 'White' Masked has been bred, in the same way that Silver Cherries are produced in the case of the Peach-faced Lovebird.

FISCHER'S LOVEBIRD – *Agapornis fischeri* (Reichenow) 1887

Fischer's Lovebirds are very similar to the Masked in their habits, but are perhaps slightly less common in collections. Painter, in America, obtained one bird during 1925 and, subsequently, a large number became available in Europe for the first time during 1926. Once acclimatized and, like the Masked, when provided with a nest-box, they are quite hardy.

Mutations

These are relatively scarce, bearing in mind the number of Fischer's which are bred annually.

1. Blue forms of Fischer's Lovebird

This mutation originated in Ronald Horsham's aviaries in South Africa. He was, in fact, attempting to breed Red Fischer's, selecting birds which had the widest distribution of orange down on to the breast; but one pair

40

produced three blue youngsters in a nest of four chicks. These birds had a grayish head with a blue body, and did not reproduce well when paired to each other. A similar mutation arose in Dr Warford's collection in San Francisco, California, in 1959. A separate blue form has also appeared in stock owned by Carl Grun, in Norco, California, during 1979, and is currently represented in collections there but the other two forms have apparently been lost.

2. Yellow forms of Fischer's Lovebird

These birds may well have been developed from Masked hybrids, but are currently the most-widely available mutation. In Australia, a Black-eyed variety, which is true yellow in color, has been bred; although even normals are quite scarce there. As a non-native species, several have been exported elsewhere, and this Australian form is known in Britain. An extremely rare Lutino mutation is also known. Monsieur Blanchard had a number of such birds in Toulouse, during 1942, but these were lost as a result of the Second World War.

3. Pieds

While in some cases this may be an acquired feature, Pied Fischer's can be bred. I have seen one example in Britain and there are probably others, certainly in Europe.

4. Other Mutations

Again, both a Cinnamon and a Pastel Blue form have been reported from Switzerland. They may have occurred as a result of previous deliberate hybridization. None of the birds concerned lived for long.

Color Combinations

It would, of course, be possible to create a silver form but, at present, this does not appear to have been carried out.

Nyasa Lovebird – *Agapornis lilianae* (Shelley) 1894
Synonyms: Nyasaland Lovebird; Lilian's Lovebird

Nyasa Lovebirds occur in flocks of up to one hundred birds, and are confined to areas close to water. Following their discovery in 1864, they were not clearly identified until 1894, and then named after Miss Lilian Sclater. Before this, in spite of their eye-ring, Nyasas were confused with the Peach-faced; subsequently, when first seen alive in Britain in 1926, the latter variety was expected until David Seth-Smith identified them as avicultural newcomers.

These lovebirds are now quite rare in British collections, although why this should be the case is not clear. Nyasas are generally prolific birds and

The Fischer's Lovebird
(*Agapornis fischeri*)

still represented in Australian and New Zealand collections. Perhaps in Europe, with their tendency to breed during the winter months, they have suffered from a higher degree of dead-in-the-shell chicks and related problems. Stock exported from Europe to Britain proved weak, which hastened the decline of the species there. Pairs are now expensive, but it is to be hoped that the surviving numbers will be increased gradually, so that they again become more widely-available. When breeding, pairs agree well if kept on a colony system but, with hindsight, might not be considered completely hardy. Therefore, as for the Madagascar Lovebird, they should be overwintered inside.

Mutations

The only genuine mutation known to exist is the Lutino. Birds of this type have also become increasingly scarce in recent years, even in Australia where the 'sport' was first bred in Adelaide during 1930. The mode of inheritance is slightly unusual, because it is an autosomal recessive mutation, and not sex-linked like the majority of other known Lutino mutations.

The first Lutino Nyasas reached Britain during 1937 and, subsequently, E.N.T. Vane built up a stock of these birds, some of which were sent to Denmark after his death in 1961. These bred well, but died out as a result of an influenza outbreak. A few remain elsewhere, however, and a separate American strain first appeared in 1940. There are also reports of blues in America, which may be genuine, or they could be hybrid

BLACK-CHEEKED LOVEBIRD – *Agapornis nigrigenis* (Sclater) 1906
Synonym: Black-faced Lovebird

This species is similar to the Nyasa in its habits, but has an even more restricted range. Black-cheeked Lovebirds were introduced to aviculture in 1907 and, during the 1920s, large numbers suddenly became available — reports suggest that they proved easy to breed. However, today these lovebirds are scarce, but pairs can be prolific. As with the Nyasa, some prefer to nest during the European winter. Because of past hybridization with other members of the White eye-ringed group, it is not always easy to obtain pure stock. Such birds are often redder on the head but, naturally, there may be a range in their coloration, with some individuals being brighter than others.

Mutations

A blue form was reported in the past, but its origins were somewhat suspect. Henning Jacobsen tells me, however, of a genuine Blue Black-cheeked, bred in 1981 in Denmark. The blue in this bird was darker on the rump, and the overall appearance most attractive. Pieds are known, but this is regarded as an acquired characteristic at present, and not a genuine mutant.

6. Exhibition

The showing of lovebirds has become increasingly popular during recent years, particularly with the increasing number of mutations. There are at present, no standards laid down for exhibition birds in Britain, although it is likely these may be developed fairly soon, specifying, for example markings in the case of pieds. At present, however, the steadiness and condition of the exhibits are the most significant features considered by judges.

Show technique

Lovebirds do not always make good exhibition birds, often retiring to the far corner of their cage when the judge or other people approach. Such behavior can invariably be traced to insufficient prior training. If the aim is to develop an exhibition stud, all birds should be made accustomed to a show cage shortly after fledging, once they are eating independently, and be given regular subsequent spells of training. They should then be used to a show cage, and people in their immediate vicinity. If a bird persists in seeking the floor of the cage, it may help to turn the cage upside down, as the roof is not flat.

Lovebirds are best exhibited in pairs but, if one member is not in top condition, only one bird should be benched, to avoid its chances being spoilt by its partner. In the case of the sexually dimorphic species, only true pairs should be shown. Apart from the condition of the plumage, which must be immaculate, the birds should be physically perfect, with all toe-nails present. Deformities, such as deviated nails or distorted beaks will be penalized. Size should also be considered as, generally, larger birds of a particular species find favor with a judge, providing they are matched in this respect. Depth of coloration is also significant and, although there is some natural variation, as seen in the case of the Peach-faced subspecies, pairs showing the deepest color are to be preferred.

Cages

At present, there is no standard with regard to show cages, although budgerigar team cages have been more widely used in Britain for lovebirds recently. Some suppliers advertise 'lovebird show cages', but birds do not have to be benched in standardized models, as is the case with budgerigars, for example. However all cages used for lovebirds must be in immaculate condition, and do not require any decoration. Bear in mind that any exposure to a sudden change in temperature can cause the birds to molt slightly and, after a show, they should only be released back into flights during a spell of good weather.

The whole training process really revolves around taming the young lovebirds from the outset, in the hope that they will later remain steady as they mature. Obviously, this is also to be recommended for breeding purposes, since the birds will be less nervous and should prove better parents.

Show entries

For a particular show, the schedule listing all classes and an entry form should be obtained, from the show secretary, as early as possible, and then carefully completed. If there is any doubt over a particular bird, it should be entered, as it can be withdrawn subsequently; late entries, after the published closing date, are never accepted.

While the exhibition side of lovebird keeping and breeding is still in its infancy, the chances of winning are perhaps higher than with other species, because the competition may well be less strong. Nevertheless, the interest and enjoyment generated by meeting others with the same hobby should be as significant as winning, and this aspect of showing should never be overlooked.

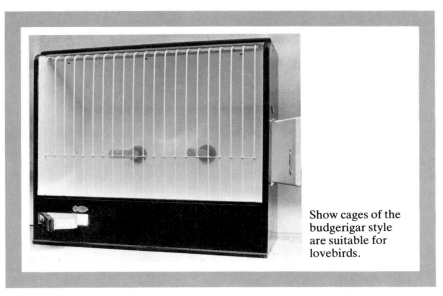

Show cages of the budgerigar style are suitable for lovebirds.

7. Health Problems

There are a variety of diseases to which lovebirds are susceptible but, generally, if kept under suitable conditions, they rarely fall ill and may live for ten years or more. If an individual is thought to be unwell, it should be transferred to a warm environment, about 30°C (85°F), and veterinary advice sought without delay. A hospital cage, with a heater or an infra-red lamp, can be used to maintain this temperature and then, following recovery, the bird should be gradually re-acclimatized.

A sick lovebird will often appear dull, and fluffed-up, as well as losing its appetite. Dark brown seed kernels in the food-pot are a sign that all is not well, since the bird is dehusking but not actually eating its seed. Weight loss, termed 'going light', can be detected by distinct hollows on either side of the breastbone in birds which have been unwell for a while. If a bacterial infection is responsible for the condition, it should respond well to the correct antibiotic therapy, providing the prescribed dose, and instructions for use are adhered to.

Cuts and Bleeding

Bleeding will usually occur if a claw has been trimmed too short; for this reason, the blood supply, visible as a thin red streak in the claw, must always be clearly located before nipping off the end of the overgrown nail. If adjoining flights are not double-wired, bleeding from foot injuries is likely to be caused by fighting through the wire.

The beak receives a partial blood supply, and there is again a risk of hemorrhage if it is not cut back carefully. Some comparison with a normal beak is useful, before actually carrying out the procedure, with a strong pair of scissors or bone clippers. In cases where bleeding is a problem, the application of a styptic pencil or a cold solution of potash alum, to the wound, should stem the blood loss.

Egg-binding

This is a potentially fatal disorder, requiring rapid treatment. It results from an egg becoming lodged in part of the reproductive tract, so it is only seen in hens which have been showing signs of breeding behavior. A shortage of calcium, chilling and immaturity of the bird concerned are all possible causes of this condition. In cases of calcium deficiency especially, the egg may only have a soft, rubbery shell.

The bird should be transferred to a warm environment, where the temperature can be maintained at about 30°C (85°F); in some cases, this alone is sufficient to ensure that the egg is passed successfully. If there is no improvement, however, it will need to be removed by other means, either directly, or following an injection of calcium borogluconate given by a vet. Such birds should not then be expected to breed for at least a year.

Enteritis and Other Digestive Problems

Crop trouble is occasionally seen in lovebirds, with the crop becoming distended and filled with frothy gas. The lovebird makes retching movements and the head feathers become stained with vomit. Treatment consists of holding the bird upside down, and carefully milking out the crop. Potassium permanganate in the drinking water, sufficient to turn it slightly pink, may help to prevent a recurrence.

Digestive infections affecting the intestines are often grouped together as 'enteritis'. Typical signs are greenish, loose droppings and loss of appetite, but early treatment with antibiotics, given in the water, is often successful in such cases.

Eye disorders

These are often first noticed when a reddening and swelling closes the eye. If both eyes are affected, this could be a sign of a general infection. Antibiotic ophthalmic ointments, applied several times daily, are often of help in curing eye infections.

Feather Disease

French molt is becoming a major problem in certain breeding establishments, affecting young birds around fledging time. They lose some or all of their flight and tail feathers, and are thus known as 'runners'. Less severely affected birds will regrow the lost feathers, and appear normal, but can often be recognized by the presence of odd, dark brownish clots of blood in the feather shafts. This should not be confused with the healthy and consistently pink colors of a normal, immature feather.

The cause of French Molt is currently unknown, but experimentally, excess vitamin E has been shown to lead to an increased incidence. Just recently, it has been suggested that the condition can be improved, and possibly prevented, by use of the antibiotic, lincomycin, but conclusive results of such therapy are not yet available.

Parasites

Red mite (*Dermanyssus gallinae*) is a relatively common parasite, living in dark areas, such as nest-boxes, and coming out to feed on the bird's blood. This can cause anemia, especially in young birds, and an overall loss of condition. All mites and lice, are easily destroyed, however, by means of a safe avian aerosol spray; while, as an additional precaution, the birds' quarters must be washed with a similar preparation. Intestinal worms, particularly roundworms, are found in lovebirds, especially those kept in aviaries with grass floors where Australian parrakeets have lived previously. The signs of infection are relatively non-specific, being a lack of vigor, with the bird appearing slightly dull and off-color. It is often possible to detect the presence of worms by examining a fresh sample of feces for their characteristic eggs; a veterinarian will assist with this task, and provide the necessary treatment. The aviary itself will need to be thoroughly disinfected to kill off any surviving eggs.

Respiratory Problems

As with enteritis, there are many possible causes for breathing disorders. Labored breathing can be recognized by irregular, exaggerated tail movements. Various fungi, bacteria and viruses can all affect the respiratory tract, and wheezing may be audible, especially at night when the birds are otherwise quiet. If the nostrils are blocked, this is indicative of sinusitis.

Lovebirds at a Glance

Generic Name	*Agapornis*
Distribution	Africa and some offshore islands
Number of Species	Nine
Size	Varies between 13−16 cm (5¼−6½ in)
Longevity	10 years or possibly longer
Sexual Dimorphism	In some cases. Hens less colorful.
Number of Eggs	3−8, rarely more.
Incubation Period	23 days. Hens sit alone, mates may join.
Chicks Leave Nest	6 weeks old or thereabouts.
Chicks Independent	About a week after leaving the nest.